Taking Shape

Seeing the Bible Whole

David Spriggs
with Mike Simmonds

Bible Society
Stonehill Green
Westlea
Swindon SN5 7DG
biblesociety.org.uk
bibleresources.org.uk

First published 2014 by The British and Foreign Bible Society.

ISBN: 978-0-564-04347-7

Production by Bible Society Resources Ltd, a wholly-owned subsidiary of The British and Foreign Bible Society
Cover and text design by Colin Hall, TypeFunction

Printed in Great Britain
BSRL/IM/2014

CONTENTS

INTRODUCTION

What this book offers

This book provides a comprehensive survey of the whole Bible. If you long to feel that you have a handle on the Bible then this is for you. It will enable you not only to work out where any individual book fits in the Bible as a collection of books but also how it contributes to the unfolding story that the Bible offers us.

Our research highlighted the need for an overview of the Bible. Opening or hearing it read in church can feel like finding ourselves transported to a strange land. We do not know the customs and the history of the peoples around us, nor do we have much idea of where we are or in which direction we are heading. This book is meant to help rescue people from chronic disorientation.

What's in the book?

In the Protestant Bible there are 39 books in the Old Testament and 27 in the New. The first four chapters – two each – are devoted to these Testaments. The Hebrew Bible is arranged differently. Many people value some additional books known as the Deuterocanon or the Apocrypha. They provide us with insights into the history and beliefs of people living in the last 300 years or so before the birth of Jesus Christ. The Deuterocanon is covered in chapter 6.

Inevitably this slim volume cannot cover anything in detail. It is a small scale map, not an A-Z! It can help provide the big picture of the Bible, not only in providing us with an initial orientation but also in areas where we already have a more detailed knowledge. If we know, say, the prophet Amos, or the Psalms in the Old Testament, or the Gospels or Romans in the New, we now see how these parts fit with the whole. The 'big picture' and more detailed knowledge complement one another.

Using the booklet

There are at least three ways to use this booklet.

1. **In a small group**. There are activities suggested in each of the first five chapters and five key Bible passages for each chapter. It would be great if the group could read and discuss at least one of these passages as well as reading the remaining four before they next meet, perhaps starting that session with sharing insights and comments on these. Working in a group, with or without a leader, means that we can help one another with aspects that some find more difficult. We can also encourage each other to keep going, right to the end.
2. **On your own**. The advantage of this approach is that you can read a few sentences of the booklet and then explore the parts of the Bible to which it relates, especially if they are unfamiliar to you or catch your interest. That is why, throughout the chapters, there are biblical references. Reading the Bible, in the context the booklet offers, will greatly enrich the experience and ensure that what is learnt 'sticks' a lot better. Some of the activities in each chapter are well suited for individual use.
3. **As a reference guide**. This booklet has been designed to be portable. So, like your mobile phone, you can always have it with you. Then, when a Bible book is mentioned – in church or wherever – you can

> have a quick look and locate where you are in the Bible's story. Of course option 3 is valid alongside 1 and 2. It is not an either...or. No one can absorb all it offers at the first reading. It is meant to become your friend, always there when you need it, or indeed when someone you know needs it.

Our prayer is that this Bible overview will help take the sense of strangeness and even fear away from the Bible. We hope that as people use it and become familiar with it they will have much greater confidence in handling the Bible for themselves, and in helping others discover that it has so much to offer us as we seek to make sense of many of life's big challenges and issues. Knowing where we are, with any book of the Bible, is a vital component. That is one reason why we have also introduced the metaphor of the Bible as a five act drama; find out more in chapter 5. The 'drama' is one in which believers are meant to get involved, filling out the Bible's story, as it were, by who they are and the way they live. Chapter 5 will help you discover what it means to have a dynamic and interactive relationship with the Bible as a whole. If chapters 1–4 and 6 provide us with our Bible road map, chapter 5 is the brochure, stimulating our imaginations to want to be involved and to discover as much as we possibly can.

The following pages will show you how the Bible's many parts fit together in time, and where events referred to are taking place. Geography always contributes to the shaping of peoples and events, so don't forget to make use of the maps provided or indeed the more detailed maps at the back of a Bible.

Additional reading

Here are a few more books which seek to cover the whole Bible. They will expand your knowledge considerably.

The Lion Handbook to the Bible, by P and D Alexander (18 Sep 2009): this is a brilliant book to take you further into the world of the Bible. It contains colour photographs, pictures and maps, introductory articles on biblical topics as well as a brief commentary for each chapter of each book of the Bible.

The Drama of Scripture – Finding our place in the biblical story, by Craig Bartholomew and Michael Goheen, (SPCK 2006), is an extended application of the 'Drama of Scripture' metaphor to the Bible. One interesting issue it raises is to what extent we should follow the biblical order, and to what extent we should follow the presupposed historical order of events or indeed the one(s) reconstructed by scholars. There is also scant attention paid to the wisdom component of the Bible. Bartholomew and Goheen have also written.

Living at the Crossroads: An Introduction to Christian Worldview (SPCK 2008). The authors seek to unpack what it means to live at a stage in the biblical drama where believers faced with modern-day issues cannot draw easily from scriptural teaching but need to rely on 'faithful improvisation', e.g. in areas like education or politics.

Tom Wright, New Testament scholar, former Bishop of Durham and creator of the 'Drama of Scripture' metaphor, has written about it in several places. One of the most extended accounts is *Scripture and the Authority of God* (SPCK 2005).

Richard Bauckham, *Scripture and Authority Today* (Grove Booklets B12 1999).

God's Big Picture (IVP 2003) and *Life's Big Questions* (IVP 2004), both by Vaughan Roberts, offer a complementary approach to this book - obviously rather larger and so with some more detail.

Essential 100, by Whitey Kuniholm (Scripture Union 2003), is the guide for those who prefer to read core chapters from the whole Bible. After a brief survey of the biblical books, there are 100 Scripture passages, each of which come with a personal commentary.

SESSION 1

GENESIS

How it all began

Genesis comes from a Greek word meaning 'beginnings'.

> 'In the beginning God created...' Genesis 1.1 (CEV)

That is how this fascinating and huge book, the Bible, begins. With such simple and profound words, the greatest story ever told gets underway. All the way through it we will be constantly reminded that, whatever else is going on, this story is ultimately about God. But don't be deceived; it is no simple story and the reality of God is far from simple! Indeed it will take the whole Bible to introduce us to God, *Yahweh Elohim*.

GENESIS
Chapters
1–2 Creation of the universe, the world and humankind by God's command
3–11 Depiction of the impact of disobedience and of God's over-arching grace to restore
12–36 Abraham, Isaac and Jacob under the promises of God
37–50 Joseph's story and how 'Israel' arrives in Egypt

5 MINUTES

Share something from your recent experience to illustrate your appreciation of our world. On balance, do you prefer nature or people?

The beginnings of the universe

Following 'God' the next word in Genesis 1.1 is 'created'. In the rest of the chapter the origin of the universe is depicted, with a clear focus on our world – where order is established effortlessly (by God's word a day at a time) and the abundance of the created world is presented as the generosity of God. Within the world the focus is on humankind, created 'to be like [God] himself' (1.27, CEV). Like a drumbeat there is the declaration that all God sees is good, very good. But the climax of this chapter is the seventh day: God rested on that day and blessed it.

We recognise that the 'origins' of the world described here are not so much a scientific account as one that highlights the order, security and essential goodness of the world but also its distinctiveness from God. Humans are there to manage and develop the earth for and with God and to join him, through worship, in celebrating the wonder of the world that God has made.

Genesis, the book of natural 'beginnings' is about other beginnings too, namely the special relationships between God and humankind, and man and woman (chapter 2). Sadly this perfect harmony is shattered in chapter 3 with the disobedience of the man and the woman (eating the forbidden fruit) and the consequential threefold breakdown of human relationships: with each other, with our Creator and with creation. Chapters 3-11 indicate the growing and intensifying consequence of this brokenness. Jealousy and anger lead to murder within the family. Evil's proliferation leads to the terrifying verdict 'Cruelty and violence have spread everywhere' (6.13, CEV). So in order to save the world God decrees the flood whilst saving Noah and his family and all the variety of animal life God had created in the boat (the ark). At each step of evil and the consequential judgement, God's forgiveness and grace are manifest too. Hence, the rainbow is God's promise that stability and productivity will be guaranteed for the future.

This cleansing flood does not end the growing disruption and violence. The building of the tower of Babel ('a tower that reaches to the sky' – Genesis 11.3, CEV) reflects the arrogance of civilisations but ends with their breakdown.

> The Lord confused their language and scattered them all over the earth.
>
> (11.8)

'The downward spiral of rebellion in Genesis 3-11 is thankfully shot through with moments of God's mercy – in promising the destruction of the serpent, in providing coverings for Adam and Eve, in giving Cain a protective mark, in saving Noah and his family, in reaffirming his blessing on creation and humanity after the flood.

Even against the backdrop of the building of Babel by those who want to "make a name" for themselves, judgment is not the last word: God does not reject the nations, but chooses one family for the sake of the nations, to bring blessing to the nations.'

A Billington, *Word for the Week: Whole Life, Whole Bible* (9/50): London: LICC (1 June 2009. anthony.billington.blogspot.co.uk/2009/06/word-for-week-whole-l-whole-bible.html)

Some people see that there are five 'genealogies' before Abraham and five after him. Genesis 2.4; 5.1-32; 6.9; 10.1-32; 11.10-26; 11.27-32; 25.12-18; 25.19-20; 36.1-5; 36.9-43.

By now we understand that this is an act of divine mercy as much as of judgement. God is committed to seeing his project of creation through to its conclusion, whatever the cost.

Intermingled with these stories which provide us with a theological understanding of the physical, social and spiritual environment as we encounter it, are accounts of the development of the human race – we call them genealogies (see chapters 5, 10, 11.10–30). They are extended family trees conveying us from the time of origins through to the conception of the nation of Israel. In a significant way they parallel the account of creation in that they focus on Abram (later known as Abraham), but at the same time they place him (and his descendants – the nation of Israel) in the widest context, the world of nations. The genealogies are important too, in that in the midst of the picture of growing disorder, they reflect the orderliness of human life. God has not lost control.

The beginnings of Israel

The rest of Genesis is then about the beginnings of Israel, her conception and gestation. God calls Abram from Ur and Haran, major cities of the Ancient Near East, to leave everything and trust in God's promise.

> Go to the land that I will show you... I will bless you and make your descendants into a great nation... Everyone on earth will be blessed because of you.
>
> Genesis 12.1–3 (CEV)

Like the rainbow, this multifaceted promise will accompany Abraham and his descendants and has a universal intention. God's promises are not only for Abraham and his immediate descendants, Isaac and Jacob, but also the people of Israel, whose story proper does not begin until Exodus (the second book of the Bible).

What follows in the next, almost 40 chapters, feels like an early version of TV soap. We follow Abraham's extended family through its joys and sorrows, its troubles and celebrations, its conflicts and resolutions. Unlike a modern soap, where the location tends to be fixed, these people are constantly on the move as they criss-cross the Ancient Near East from Iraq to Egypt. Such a dynamic is important, for these people are restless, looking for a homeland. Even more of a contrast with any 'soap' is that the 'director' is God!

Abraham

Chapters 12-23: Abraham acts deceitfully to try and stay alive when he and his clan go to Egypt during a famine; he seeks to pass his wife Sarai (later known as Sarah) off as his sister, which gets everyone (including the Pharaoh) in trouble. Abraham's nephew, Lot, together with his family, separates from them because of quarrels sparked by water and food shortages (13). Lot ends up in Sodom and Gomorrah, which leads to more troubles (18-19). Yet through this we discover more of the nature of God as Abraham pleads for mercy on those cities. God's response to Abraham indicates that he does not want to use destructive judgement and he is always acting for a positive outcome. An even more important theme is that of Abraham's heir. Abraham tries to fix the childlessness issue himself by having a child with his concubine, Hagar (16), but that all goes wrong and leads to ongoing turmoil. Finally, as a divine gift, Isaac is born. All seems settled; the fulfilment of God's promise is underway. Then God challenges Abraham to sacrifice Isaac (22). The tension is paramount, but God provides the substitute - a ram - at the last minute. We learn God must be more of a priority than our well-being or even our perception of his promises. He can be trusted to deliver on his promises.

Isaac and Jacob

Chapters 24-36: The story continues through the next two generations, with Isaac and his son Jacob being the chief characters. The section opens with a beautiful story of how Isaac finds his wife, Rebekah. Abraham sends a trusted servant back to his homeland and through prayer and guile discovers the beautiful Rebekah and persuades her father to let him return to Canaan where Abraham is settling down. As with Abraham, so with Isaac, apparent childlessness becomes an issue. Eventually, as the result of prayer, twins are born. What follows is a story of sibling rivalry between Jacob and his brother Esau. The trigger is that Rebekah helps Jacob deceive the now-blinded Isaac into giving him the family blessing and inheritance. Understandably Esau is wrathful and Jacob has to flee to stay alive. He has amazing encounters with God (28 and 32) but in between is deceived by Laban, his father-in-law, and ends up marrying two wives – Laban's daughters – and having to work as a kind of bonded slave for 14 years (29). Here he learns the hard way the price of deception. In the end there is a marvellous scene of reconciliation between Esau and Jacob in chapter 33, but this is followed by the rape of one of Jacob's daughters and the punishment of the perpetrators. He ends up with 12 children from four 'wives' but family rivalry persists.

Jacob's sons

Chapters 37–50: Rachel was Jacob's favourite wife and her children, Joseph and Benjamin, were Jacob's favourites, with Joseph being his special son (37.3). Joseph dreams of his superiority and unsurprisingly his brothers are angry. Eventually this leads to him being sold as a slave into Egypt. The other sons cause the elderly Jacob immense grief by leading him to think that Joseph is dead.

Interspersed with the fascinating and richly textured narrative of Joseph, there is another sad story of the oppression of a woman, Tamar, by one of Jacob's sons, Judah, and his sons (38). It involves broken promises, several deaths and much deception, in order to arrive at a just solution. The story is even more puzzling in that the central tragic character, Judah, is the very one used by God to preserve Joseph's life. In some ways this strange episode is a microcosm of God's own challenge, how to bring about redemptive justice in a very corrupt and confused world.

Once in Egypt, Joseph starts his social climbing. Although Potiphar, his master and a leading military commander, trusts him a great deal, his wife is obsessed with Joseph and affronted when he refuses her advances. This lands Joseph in prison, where once again he rises to a privileged position.

Again dreams play a part. Joseph interprets dreams which his fellow prisoners, the royal butler (or wine steward) and cook, have had. The butler will be freed, the other executed. Joseph asks the wine steward to seek clemency for himself from the king. The butler forgets, until the king has a perplexing couple of dreams as well. Then the wine steward recalls his prison encounter. Joseph is summoned from prison by the king and interprets his dreams. Seven years of bumper harvests will be followed by seven devastating years of famine. Joseph is made second authority in the land and told to sort out the problem. He does this with incredible acumen ensuring that Egypt is not only well prepared for the famine itself but also in a powerful trading position.

Thus when famine reaches Canaan, Joseph's brothers go to Egypt to buy food. Unbeknown to them it is Joseph they meet. He comes up with a series of plans which ensure that eventually his brothers admit their wickedness and his father Jacob, together with the extended family, move to settle in Egypt. One of the most memorable lines in the entire account is Joseph's address to his brothers when he reveals his identity – the moment when they could expect a death sentence:

> Don't worry or blame yourselves for what you did. God is the one who sent me ahead of you to save lives.
>
> Genesis 45.5 (CEV)

But even more profoundly, perhaps expressing the ultimate theological perspective,

> Do not be afraid! Am I in the place of God? Even though you intended to do harm to me, God intended it for good.
>
> Genesis 50.19,20 (NRSV)

Through this one book of the Bible, we have journeyed far, from the creation of the universe through to the embryonic Israel, now settled in Egypt under divine and royal protection. But is Egypt the land God promised Abraham?

Suggestions for reflection

Using the verse below, reflect on the events covered in the book of Genesis.

Everything was created by him,
everything in heaven
and on earth,
everything seen and unseen,
including all forces
and powers,
and all rulers
and authorities.
All things were created
by God's Son,
and everything was made
for him.

Colossians 1.16 (CEV)

1. What does Genesis 1 add to this 'description' from the New Testament?
2. What does the New Testament verse cover that you do not find in Genesis 1?
3. Write down some key words to describe your relationship with the Creator God made known through Jesus Christ.

Bible encounter

Read Genesis 22.1–19. Consider how important this story is for the book of Genesis and beyond. What questions might it raise for a contemporary reader? Perhaps pray for people who have issues with infertility or with adolescent children.

Group discussion questions

Half the group read Genesis 3

- To what extent do you think this chapter is important for bridging between Genesis 1 (the creation of the world) and the world as we experience it today? Does the chapter explain the mystery of sin? Focus on the characteristics of God as they are portrayed in this chapter.

The other half read Genesis 24

- This chapter was described as a beautiful story. List the ways in which it encourages faith in God. Voice any concerns you might have about the method of finding a bride.

Key readings

Genesis 1.1-2.4
Genesis 11.27-12.20
Genesis 45.1-20
Genesis 3.1-24
Genesis 22.1-19
Genesis 45.1-20

SESSION 2

EXODUS TO MALACHI

The story of Israel

This session covers a vast amount of the Bible. It sweeps over four books of the Pentateuch (Exodus–Deuteronomy), the historical books (Joshua–Ezra), takes a brief look at the Wisdom literature and Psalms and ends with the four great prophetic compositions. What riches; what a challenge.

Exodus-Deuteronomy
The journey from Egypt to the edge of Canaan

Joshua-Nehemiah
The journey from tribal confederacy through monarchy to exile and return to Jerusalem

Isaiah-Malachi
The four great prophetic collections of Isaiah, Jeremiah, Ezekiel and 'The Twelve'

The Writings
Esther, Job, Psalms, Proverbs, Ecclesiastes, Song of Solomon

5 MINUTES

Discuss together a) which parts you know best and least; b) which is your favourite verse or chapter.

Exodus to Deuteronomy

Exodus begins with Israel as slaves in Egypt, continues with God's call of Moses to lead his people to freedom, the conflict with Pharaoh and the plagues sent by God as Pharaoh rejects God's command to let the Hebrew slaves leave Egypt. Following the Passover – through which Israelite families were spared the fate that befell the Egyptians, when their firstborn sons died – the story moves on to the

Israelites' dramatic escape across the Red Sea. Eventually God initiates the covenant with his people at Mount Sinai, including the Ten Commandments, and provides the instructions for the construction of the Tent of Meeting or Tabernacle. There are many laws for the conduct of worship and some details about festivals. Even within this one book there are already stories of people falling away from God, e.g. even while Moses is on Mount Sinai receiving the precious commandments from God, the people tire of waiting and build a golden bull for their worship (Exodus 32).

Leviticus to Numbers provide many stories and laws as well as detailing the tribal and priestly family structures. In addition to many stories about God's miraculous protection and provision for his people, we gain insights about their fickleness and learn of their encounters and frequent conflicts with other tribes as they journey towards the Land of Canaan. As they are poised to enter the Promised Land, areas are allocated to each of the tribes. Interestingly and yet strangely this section of the Bible ends with a decision about inheritance laws and married women.

Deuteronomy presents itself as Moses' speech to the tribes as they prepare to enter their 'promised land' (Deuteronomy 11.11). Much of it serves as a review of their desert wanderings following the escape from Egypt. Deuteronomy constantly challenges God's people to remember and to hear, that is, take notice of the past in order to learn the lessons and live appropriately as God's people. The book ends with God presenting the blessings for obedience, and the curses for disobedience and for breaking the covenant. Eventually, Moses blesses the 12 tribes and dies. In summary, Israel's God is unique (33.26), Israel is unique (33.29) and Moses is unique (34.10–12). In Deuteronomy, the mountain where the Ten Commandments are given and the covenant is established is also called Horeb or Sinai. These are alternative names for the same area.

Joshua to Nehemiah

These 'historical books' cover the period from about 1150–400 BC. They depict Israel entering and conquering the land and then scattering to their allocated tribal areas. Judges covers the period of settlement and continues the theme of Israel's waywardness. Their departure from God's laws leads to oppression by enemies who in turn are subdued by God- appointed leaders who rally groups of tribes together. We are also introduced to the Philistine traders and settlers who vie with Israel for the land. The book of Ruth presents a different insight into this period and through the family tree connects the heroine with the birth of King David.

Israel then moves from this spasmodic tribal leadership to a more cohesive nation ruled by kings. Saul is the transition king followed by David, Israel's most famous leader, David extended the territorial boundaries and established Jerusalem as his capital city, he also prepares the way for his son, Solomon, to build the temple in Jerusalem.

Solomon extends the 'empire' by treaty, trade and marriage – at a price: Israel's worship is infiltrated by foreign influences. After Solomon's death the 12-tribe nation splits into two. The southern part (often known as Judah) remains as the Davidic kingdom, the rest (the 10 northern tribes usually referred to as 'Israel') have their own kings. Both kingdoms, but especially Israel, are squeezed by more powerful empires such as Assyria and, later, Babylon to the east and Egypt to the south.

One strategy for combating these 'superpowers' was to work in alliances with the surrounding nations or even Israel and Judah joining forces. These partnerships were rarely helpful or adequate. Eventually in 721 the Assyrians invade and conquer Israel. Judah continues but falls to the Babylonians by the beginning of the sixth century; in AD 586 Jerusalem is stormed and the political, commercial and religious leaders are deported to Babylon; this is the time of Exile.

Beyond exile

The final historical period is reflected in the works of 1 and 2 Chronicles, Ezra and Nehemiah. Chronicles covers the same period as the books of Kings; indeed, from 1 Chronicles 10 onwards it often incorporates whole sections. But it has its own distinct perspective. Its main concern is with Judah and Jerusalem. It has a strong focus on the worship in the temple and the power of worship even in military campaigns (e.g. 2 Chronicles 20). It also concludes with the edict of Cyrus permitting the Jewish exiles to return from Babylon to Jerusalem. Ezra provides an account of this return, the restoration of worship in Jerusalem and the rebuilding of the temple. The challenges and significance of this project are important features of the two 'minor' prophets Haggai and Zechariah (see Ezra 5.1–2). Nehemiah is a more personal account. Having held an important post in the Persian royal court, Nehemiah uses this connection to obtain resources and permission for the rebuilding of the walls of Jerusalem and, thereby, the community of God's people.

Daniel and Esther provide reflective stories on the situation for those in exile, and also served to inspire people in the 400 years between the Old and New Testaments.

Prophecy, wisdom and priesthood

Three streams of spiritual direction and nourishment flow through this period. The first is the prophetic. Indeed Samuel–Kings are known as 'the former prophets', because what they describe is not secular history, but one through which God intervenes in warning, encouragement, regime change, and sometimes deliverance, through the words and deeds of the prophets like Elijah and Elisha (ninth century BC), whose stories are part of the people's history. But we also have four collections of prophecy, often known as the writing prophets. These are Isaiah of Jerusalem (Southern Kingdom around 700 BC), Jeremiah (Southern Kingdom around 600 BC), Ezekiel (Southern Kingdom and Babylon around 575 BC) and a collection of smaller works known as the minor prophets. These span the period from the eighth century BC to maybe even as late as 250 BC and include Amos and Hosea (Northern Kingdom), Micah (Northern and Southern Kingdom) and Habakkuk, Zechariah and Malachi. Each addresses their contemporary situations. They speak, often directly in God's name, to a changing historical situation and call the people to leave their compromised ways of life and return whole-heartedly to God. If they refuse to repent, they will find themselves rejected by God and politically crushed. The minor prophets also offer hope for those who repent because God's grace is stronger than his judgement.

Although known as the writing prophets, most of their messages were spoken initially and then written down by their followers, or under their dictation. In some cases it seems probable that their followers added further passages (see Jeremiah 36; note especially the last verse). This is particularly likely with the later chapters of Isaiah (40–65), which seem to reflect a Babylonian and post-exilic context, rather than late eighth century Jerusalem.

Amos, probably the first of the writing prophets, indicates that his role was a response to God's call. He warns the northern tribes, particularly around Samaria, of the coming judgement of God for their failure to care for the poor. Hosea probably comes a little later and his critique is of the people's involvement in Baal worship.

Isaiah focuses on the holiness of God and the call to holiness for his people. Based mainly in Jerusalem he is responding to different aspects of God's covenant, relating to King David and the protection of Jerusalem in the face of the Assyrian invasions. Jeremiah tries to challenge the people as they await God's judgement on them through the Babylonians. Ezekiel picks up on this situation but reflects the context of Exile and ends with a vision of a restored community and temple; the former was also promised by Jeremiah. Habakkuk wrestles with the problem of how God can use the Babylonians to punish Israel despite their exceptional cruelty.

Oracles
are verbal pronouncements spoken by humans but often with the implicit claim to have divine authority or to be revelatory.
The phrase 'Oracles against the nations' is often used by scholars for this genre, e.g. J.L. Mays *Amos*, SCM, 1969, contexts page.

The prophetic writings include 'oracles against the nations'. Major collections of these are found in Isaiah 13–23, Jeremiah 46–51 and Ezekiel 25–32. Amos 1–2 also makes use of them, albeit in a distinctive way: as a foil for his condemnation of Israel. Oracles reoccur in other places in the 'minor prophets'. It is not easy to understand their role in prophecy.

The second stream is preserved in Psalms – Israel's worship songs. The psalms cover everything from temple liturgies, through to songs of confession, complaint and lament. Many were primarily for corporate use, initially in the Jerusalem temple, but they can also be deeply personal and reflective. The officials who facilitated temple worship were the priests (supported by the Levites) who oversaw the sacrifices at the regular festivals and ceremonies. These were intended to enable people to maintain their relationship with God during times when they were ritually impure (such as childbirth, menstruation, illnesses and death) and in spite of human failure, faithlessness to God, ethical sinfulness and compromise.

Finally the wisdom material shows that Israel was constantly seeking to discern God and his purposes in everyday life and pass these insights on. The book of Proverbs is the clearest example. Other wisdom material wrestles with issues such as God's righteousness and human suffering (Job) and the concern that life can seem ultimately pointless (Ecclesiastes). Although such material clearly has connections with wisdom writings in other cultures, it is still distinct. One of its positional statements is that it is the fear of the Lord which is the beginning or foundation for wisdom (see Proverbs 1.7; 3.5–8). We can also note that it openly recognises connections with other cultures (1 Kings 10.1–13, Job 1.3, Proverbs 31.1–8). Thus wisdom serves as a bridge between the believing community of Israel and other nations.

Messianic hopes

Interwoven with this wide ranging material we find the expectation of a new God-given future. Sometimes this is expressed in terms of a 'new covenant' (e.g. Isaiah 9.7; Jeremiah 31.31-33; Ezekiel 36.25-26; Hosea 11.1), sometimes of a return to paradise (e.g. Isaiah 11.6-9; Ezekiel 47.1-12) and perhaps most frequently in terms of the restoration of a God-given king – often linked to King David (e.g. Isaiah 9-7, 11.1-5, 55.3; Jeremiah 23.5, 33.17; Ezekiel 34.23-25). There are also hints of a wider vision, when Israel will be a light for the nations (Isaiah 49.6, compare with 19.23–25). These future hopes point the way, from a Christian perspective, to the coming of Jesus.

Group discussion

The time span covered by the historical and the prophetic books is around 800 years. That is a great deal of time for any nation! Think of what has happened to your country in the last 800 years. Each member of the group notes down five significant events or changes. Then share these.

1. How similar or different are the lists?
2. What factors may have influenced your selection?
3. What factors might have influenced the history writing and prophecies in Israel?

Read the following passages (either out loud as a group, or quietly): Isaiah 9.6–7; Jeremiah 31.31–34; Jeremiah 33.14–18; Ezekiel 37.11–14; Hosea 14.4–7.

1. Discuss how you think these 'prophesies' are, or are not, fulfilled in Jesus. Alternatively allocate one passage to each of four sub-groups and share your findings.
2. What guides us towards our views?

Bible encounter

Arrange the names in the word cloud as a list (in the order they first appear in the Bible). Have a go without any

helps. Then look in your Bibles (perhaps with the help of a concordance). Our attempt can be found on page 46.

- What do you notice about the gender ratio?
- What does this suggest to you about the world of the Bible?

Suggestions for reflection

Read 1 Kings 10.1–29. Reflect on what this tells us about the importance of Israel's status in the reign of Solomon, e.g. by making a list of the things which impressed the Queen of Sheba. How important is it for today that we have Christians who can impress people in authority?

Key readings

Deuteronomy 5
Judges 6
1 Kings 10.1–29
Isaiah 6
Jeremiah 31.16–36

SESSION 3

MATTHEW TO JOHN

The Good News of Jesus Christ

For Christians the books we know as the Gospels of Matthew, Mark, Luke and John are the most treasured literature in the world, because they tell us almost all we know about the birth, ministry, death and resurrection of Jesus.

Most of his life Jesus lived in Nazareth, a small town in the north of Galilee. His public ministry, lasting up to three years, moved between Galilee and Jerusalem.

The first three Gospels present a similar perspective and are called the Synoptic Gospels. The fourth, John, takes a rather different approach.

Matthew
the most Jewish Gospel contains extended teaching of Jesus and the only references to 'church'

Mark
action packed and rather elementary Greek

Luke
intended for an educated Gentile audience, great storytelling and compassion for the marginalised

John
a different approach to the other Gospels, focusing more on Jesus in Jerusalem

5 MINUTES

Recall one of your favourite stories from the Gospels and share it with someone in your group. Then listen to theirs.

Presenting the origins of Jesus

Matthew

Matthew and Luke provide us with the background to Jesus' birth, but in different ways. Matthew begins with a very structured genealogy which emphasises the link of Jesus to

Abraham (the patriarch who received God's promise that all nations would be blessed) and David (Israel's paradigm king, whose reign is interpreted prophetically, pointing to God's future deliverer). Matthew goes on to present the conception of Jesus from Joseph's perspective utilizing Old Testament quotations. This emphasis on the 'fulfilment of Scripture' (e.g. 1.22; 2.5, 15, 18; 3.3; 4.14; 13.35; 25.26) is a hallmark of Matthew's account, so his Gospel is frequently considered to be written for a Jewish audience. He continues by recounting the birth of Jesus, the visit of the Magi, the flight into Egypt by Joseph, Mary and Jesus to escape the wrath of Herod, and the massacre of the other Bethlehem infants by Herod's soldiers. We also learn of Joseph and his family's eventual return to Nazareth. All this takes place by the end of chapter 2!

Luke

Luke focuses on Mary's side of the family, with stories about John the Baptist's conception and birth to her cousin Elizabeth, as well as the visit of the Angel Gabriel to Mary explaining about the divine conception of her son. These early chapters are filled with prayers and songs that are resonant with Old Testament allusions, rather than Scripture quoted as prophetic fulfilment. Luke's birth account focuses on the Roman context (his introduction explains that his Gospel is written for a Gentile: 1.1-3), the angelic messengers (he refers to angels a lot) and the visit of the shepherds to the infant Jesus. It is Luke alone that gives us a small glimpse into the childhood and early adolescence of Jesus. None of the Gospels provide much insight about his early adult years; they are not biographies as we understand them, but present us with those aspects of the life of Jesus which enable us to appreciate who he is – Son of Man, Messiah (or Christ), Son of God – and what he came to accomplish (Saviour).

Mark

Mark starts his account with John the Baptist's call for the Jewish nation to repent, which prepares for the arrival of Jesus as an adult, ready to be baptised, receive the Holy Spirit's endorsement and then experience temptations by the devil.

John

John, on the other hand, begins his Gospel with the origins of 'the Word' in the Godhead and his incarnation in a much more allusive way:

> The Word became a human being and lived here with us.
>
> John 1.14 (CEV)

This 'Word' seems to reflect Old Testament language about God's word bringing about creation, his address to Israel through law, promise and prophecy, but also later Jewish thought and Greek understandings too. In Greek, 'Word' also indicates meaning, reason and the essential nature of the universe. John seeks to fuse these different understandings to indicate that Jesus is 'the Saviour of the world' (John 4.42, compare with 3.16–18).

The differences in presenting the origins of Jesus are rather typical of the whole of the Gospels. But they also indicate that the four perspectives provide us with a rich collage from which to gain a more comprehensive understanding of who Jesus was and is.

Comparing the Gospels

Matthew

Matthew's Gospel has five main sections, possibly mirroring the first five books of the Old Testament. These sections are marked off by a concluding formula (see 7.28; 11.1; 13.53; 19.1; 26.1). This, together with a strong emphasis on the teaching of Jesus, leads some scholars to think that Matthew sought to present him as the new Moses. The 'Sermon on the Mount' is the most extended and best-known collection of Jesus' sayings (5–7). It includes the Beatitudes – a series of short statements indicating who is 'blessed' or 'happy', that is those whose lives are particularly pleasing to God. There is teaching on anger, divorce, revenge and our attitude to possessions. More elusive teaching is found in Jesus' parables – imaginative stories which can tease open our minds to him afresh. However, if people were resistant to Jesus (perhaps because he threatened their status), these stories and imaginative sayings puzzled them even more. This is roughly what Jesus' parable about a farmer (or sower) and four different soils indicates (see Matthew 13.1–23).

Jesus' parables can be found in all the synoptic Gospels, as can frequent mention of the 'kingdom of God', both within parables and elsewhere. The kingdom signifies God's rule and its recognition. It is already happening in heaven and Jesus is bringing it to human life on earth. This concept is central to Jesus and his teaching.

The kingdom of God

Means the kingship or rule rather than the territory.

Is the same as the kingdom of heaven (in Matthew).

Occurs frequently in the Synoptic Gospels but only twice in John 3.3,5.

It is equivalent to God's will being done (Matthew 6. 10).

It is both present (in heaven) and to come on earth (it is strongly associated with Jesus e.g. Mark 1.1,15; Luke 11. 20; 17. 20–21) but it is also still to come (Mark 9.1).

People can seek the kingdom (Luke 12.31), it is also a gift (Luke 12.32) which people can receive (Mark 10.15) or enter (Matthew 5. 20) .

Mark

While Mark's Gospel also includes teaching, it is far more energetic. One of Mark's favourite words is 'immediately' or as it is translated in the CEV 'as soon as' (e.g. 1-8; 3.16). This gives a great sense of urgency: Jesus gathers his 12 disciples (perhaps he chose 12 to reflect the 12 scattered tribes of Israel, which were expected to be restored at the time of the coming of the Messiah); he performs many miracles, frequently of healing and delivering people from demonic oppression, but sometimes over nature, such as calming the storm or feeding the crowd (4.35–41; 6.30–44); and often Jesus antagonises the religious leaders on the way. Jesus travels from Galilee, his own region, through to Jerusalem, where he will be crucified. But he does not head for Jerusalem until Peter has affirmed that he knows Jesus to be the 'Messiah' (in Greek this is 'The Christ'; see 8.27–30). Almost all of Mark can be found in Matthew and Luke's Gospels as well, which has suggested to many scholars that Mark was written first and used by Matthew and Luke as the structure for their own accounts of Jesus.

Luke

Luke's Gospel aimed to provide an orderly account and depended on other attempts to describe the life of Jesus (Luke 1.1–4). Luke is very sensitive to the marginalised (see 4.16–30), including the poor, women and Gentiles (non-Jews). His remarkable gift for storytelling comes out in some of the parables, which are unique to him (10.25–37; 15.11–32), and in the way he depicts people's encounters with Jesus (19.1–10; 24.13–35). Luke also emphasises prayer, both Jesus' own and his teaching about it. Mission is more strongly

The helper
There is a considerable variety of words used for the 'paraclete' – this being more or less a transliteration of the Greek. Here is a selection of translations of 'paracletos' in John 14.26

- KJV - comforter
- RSV – counsellor
- NRSV - advocate
- NIV – advocate to help you
- JB – advocate, counsellor or protector
- The Message – friend
- GNB – the helper
- CEV – who will help you
- ESV – helper, advocate or counsellor

Literally the word means 'someone called to one's side'. It was frequently used in a legal context either as an advocate, intercessor or as a witness (though in John 15.26 which has a legal flavour the Holy Spirit acts in a prosecuting rather than defence capacity). It thus came to mean someone who was on your side

underlined by Luke too (see 9.1–6 and 10.1–24), which prepares for his second volume: the Acts of the Apostles.

John

John's Gospel prefers the word 'signs' to 'miracles', as he brings out more directly the meaning of these events. The 'signs' are often associated with strong claims by Jesus such as 'I am the light of the world' (8.12, NRSV) or 'I am the bread of life' (6.35, NRSV). Many of these signs are unique to John's Gospel, although the feeding of the 5,000 occurs in them all. This Gospel seems to focus on Jerusalem rather more than the others. It conveys teaching given exclusively to the disciples which has a more intimate, even mystical, flavour (see chapters 13–16). Here we find the most direct teaching about the Holy Spirit, described as helper, or 'other comforter/encourager' (see 14.15–26; 15.26–27; 16.4–15; 20.21–23). Luke's focus on the Holy Spirit resembles John's somewhat, and there are other similarities with the Gospel of John (see Luke 1.15-35; 4.1,14,18; 10.21; 11.13; 24.49). These similarities are emphases, not absolutes; for instance, Matthew and Mark also mention the Holy Spirit at Jesus' baptism.

The last week

All the Gospels pay special attention to the last week of Jesus' life as he enters Jerusalem. They devote up to 40 per cent of their narratives to this crucial period. The coverage includes teaching; most notably in the 'Synoptics' where large passages deal with the 'end times', including the destruction of the temple in Jerusalem, the heart of Judaism – see Matthew 24–25, Mark 13, Luke 21. John concentrates on Jesus' last message to his disciples, conflict with the Jewish authorities, the final Passover meal, the trials and crucifixion of Jesus and his resurrection, heralded by angelic beings and experienced by the disciples through their encounters with the risen Jesus. As with his birth narratives, the resurrection encounters vary considerably, with Mark's account being truncated and relating no actual encounters but only the fact that Jesus' grave was empty. The resurrection encounters are important in establishing the authenticity of the Christians' claim that Jesus was alive again, showing us that the reality of this resurrected Jesus includes both continuity with the earthly, pre-crucified Jesus (he has wounds, he eats food, he is recognisable) and some discontinuity (he might not always be recognisable and he can pass through locked doors).

In Matthew and Luke, Jesus makes it very clear that the disciples are to continue his ministry, but on a global stage (Matthew 28.18–20; Luke 24.46–48) and that his post-resurrection appearances are for a limited time only.

and in this sense a legal friend. Outside the legal context it was someone who helped you with an overwhelming task. The word from which it is derived also means to encourage and challenge, for instance of soldiers going into battle. This may be reflected in the use in the New Testament with respect to prophetic preaching.

Bible encounter

Read Mark 1.1–39, note all the places that are mentioned, including regions, towns, rivers and lakes.

Now find these on a map (either in a Bible or via download). Mark the places mentioned and do an online search to find out more about any that interest you. If you have time, read through the whole of Mark's Gospel and continue this exercise.

Group discussion questions

Divide Luke's Gospel up, giving each member of the group a few chapters. Then each person scans their chapters and notes down the people who meet Jesus.

Share your findings. What does this suggest about the availability of Jesus? Did he exclude anyone?

Suggestions for reflection

What does Luke 24.1–43 tell us about the resurrection of Jesus? What was Jesus like? Who saw what? How significant was the resurrection for the disciples? Are there any features in these accounts that puzzle you? Which of the people in these stories would you have liked to be? Share your answer with the rest of the group.

Key readings

MATTHEW 2.1–23
MATTHEW 5.1–20
MARK 1.1–39
LUKE 23.13–56
JOHN 20.11–31

SESSION 4

ACTS TO REVELATION

The Church living out Jesus' life

This final section of our Bible begins with the story of the early days of the Church – or part of it. We know it as the Acts of the Apostles.

Acts is followed by 13 letters of different sizes, attributed to the Apostle Paul, mostly sent to churches but sometimes to individuals.

After Paul's letters you'll find another group of letters, including some from Peter and John, who were part of the original group of 12 disciples.

Session 4 concludes with the book of Revelation, which appears to depict the end of time as we know it: a new creation – heaven come down to earth.

5 MINUTES

Read through 1 Corinthians chapter 13 and try to recall times when you heard this passage read. Next, discuss other contexts in which you think it could be helpful. Discuss why Paul wrote the passage in the first place and consider whether its use today – often at weddings and funerals – is appropriate.

The Acts

The Acts of the Apostles begins this way:

> Theophilus, I first wrote to you about all that Jesus did and taught from the very first.
>
> Acts 1.1 (CEV)

Acts 1.1 connects Acts with the Gospel of Luke. In Acts, Luke carries on the story of the impact Jesus continued to have and the way the disciples carried out his directive to be witnesses in Jerusalem, in all Judea, in Samaria, and everywhere in the world (1.8). Once the first group of believers have received the promised Holy Spirit, things really start to happen. First, in Jerusalem, a large crowd, representing many nations of the world who have come to the temple for Pentecost, hear the good news about Jesus, repent, are baptised and join the Christian community. Rapidly – sometimes by divine direction, sometimes by persecution – the Christians spread out. Jerusalem, however, remains the spiritual centre for quite a while. The Church has to cope with organisational challenges brought about by growth, potential divisions, deceit and persecution, as well as tough choices about accepting, as full Christians, Gentiles who have not first become Jews. Things come to a head in Acts chapter 15: at the 'Council of Jerusalem' the churches agree to accept Gentiles as full Christians with only minimal, Jewish requirements; circumcision and submission to most Jewish laws and rites are not required.

At each new step God is seen to take charge, indicating the way ahead as he breaks into people's lives. Initially Peter leads the mission dispersal, but eventually Saul, who was a key persecutor, is miraculously converted (his Damascus moment), is renamed Paul and then takes centre stage as the Gospel spreads through the ancient world. Eventually he ends up as a prisoner in Rome; some think that the main purpose of Acts was to show to the authorities that Christians in general – and Paul in particular – are law-abiding, beneficial citizens of Rome. Whether this is right or

Acts provides us with an historical and geographical picture of the spread of the Gospel.

There are 13 letters attributed to Paul, written to churches and leaders.

There are other letters, Hebrews and shorter ones by Peter, James (the brother of Jesus rather than the disciple) and John.

Revelation belongs to a type of literature known as apocalyptic. It portrays the prophecies given by Jesus about seven churches and the events of the times understood as leading to God's renewal of all creation.

not, it serves to remind us that, fulsome as the account of the spread of the good news of Jesus through the ancient world is, there are many aspects of this development that are not covered. For example, we do not hear about Thomas's or most of the other disciples' missionary activities, let alone the larger group of 120 (see Acts 1.15). We have only hints about the ministry of ordinary Christians as they escaped persecution or travelled with business.

Paul's Letters

Romans and Corinthians

It is indeed Rome (or Christians in Rome) to which Paul's first and most influential letter was written. In this he explains how he sees the world in rebellion against God but how God has acted through the death of Christ to redeem, ransom and rescue fallen humanity. This process is related to 'making us right' or righteous through faith, that is trust in God's 'rescue initiative' in Jesus.

Chapter 8 is a pivotal chapter exploring the role of the Holy Spirit in our lives and assuring us of the supremacy of God's love.

This letter also contains Paul's attempt to wrestle with understanding how Gentiles could be incorporated into God's saving purposes first given to Abraham and also how, in this changed spiritual world, the Jews can still be properly fitted into God's plan. The final chapters of Romans were to help Christians understand how to live appropriately.

Pauline Letters (those in bold) are reckoned to give us the clearest picture of Paul's teachings, beliefs and practices)

Romans
1,2 Corinthians
Galatians
Ephesians
Philippians
Colossians
1,2 Thessalonians
1,2 Timothy
Titus
Philemon

The next 'two' letters (they may contain parts of four) are addressed to the Christian church in Corinth, where a very mixed social and moral group were requiring guidance about proper Christian living both in their society and the Christian community. Here we are given insight into the worship of the churches (1 Corinthians 11–14) and the centrality of the resurrection of Jesus for our faith and life (chapter 15). Among other things 2 Corinthians shows that Paul's ministry was often under attack as well as indicating something of his personal struggles and suffering.

Galatians to Thessalonians

The next group of letters are all much smaller and were sent to churches when Paul could not go himself, often because he was in prison. As with the Corinthian letters, they are often responding to questions, issues and even practical matters like financial gifts that the churches had sent to Paul. They show us insights into the heart of the Gospel as it was explained in the Roman Empire and the impact that Gospel was to make on people's individual, family and civic lives. There seem to be some parallels with the ethical teaching of Greek philosophers, especially the Stoics, but the tone is different. Life is lived out of relationship with Christ, and is essentially an act of response to the generosity of God in rescuing us from the kingdom of darkness and bringing us into his kingdom of light (Colossians 1.12–14; see also Acts 26.18 and 1 Thessalonians 1.9). The Christian life is only made possible through the transforming help of the Holy Spirit – God's 'down payment' reminding us of our final transformation when 'the present age' is brought to an end by the intervention of the glorified Christ (Ephesians 1.12–14). Each letter has its own special emphasis, for instance, Galatians relates to Christian freedom and Philippians to joy. All of them are infused with Paul's prayers of thankfulness. Through them we get fascinating, albeit incomplete, glimpses of the developing early church, as well as a suggestive array of metaphors by which Paul indicates the nature of the Christian community (e.g. 1 Corinthians 3.9; Ephesians 4.4; Philippians 2.15).

The final set of letters normally associated with Paul is addressed to individuals like Timothy and Titus, providing support and guidance to those leading in local church communities. As with Ephesians and Colossians, they indicate that the church is becoming more structured. They encourage diligence and Christ-likeness. The shortest one, sent to Philemon, was about how to handle his slave who had run away but, having become a Christian, was now returning to him.

It is difficult to be sure about the dates and so the order in which Paul's letters were written. Generally Galatians is considered early, as are 1 & 2 Thessalonians; Ephesians and Colossians came later.

The biblical order is probably not the chronological order.

Hebrews to Jude

Hebrews stands out from other letters. Most people do not think Paul wrote it, because it is very different in most respects from his letters. As well as being written in Greek of a very high quality, it engages with the Old Testament in a distinctive way. It explores who Jesus is and what he does by comparing him to Moses as well as priests such as Aaron and Melchizedek. Hebrews underlines the complete supremacy of Jesus as God's Son, exhorting Christians to live in ways that honour him, and not to give in to the pressures on them, including persecution. Some passages are particularly intense, including the famous chapter 11 that lists the heroes of the faith (see Hebrews 1.1–4, 11.1–3 and 13.20–21).

The letters of James, Peter, John and Jude complete this collection. We can relate them to different parts of the growing Christian communities, and each adds something to a deep grasp of the good news of Jesus. James challenges people to integrate their beliefs and their behaviour. Peter constantly calls people to live holy lives as God's new people and to draw inspiration from the life and death of Jesus. John is concerned to affirm the full humanity of Jesus (he was probably tackling ideas which saw Jesus as some kind of 'spiritual' manifestation of God rather than God as fully human) and to encourage his communities to live lives of Christ-like love. Jude warns against false teachers who present themselves as Christian.

Revelation

Many people find this book perplexing and strange. Also referred to as Apocalypse, it is full of imagery of beasts and violent battles and its structure mesmerises us if we try to unravel it as a linear story. We may also be aware that some extreme writings and positions about the 'end times' claim to derive from Revelation.

This is sad in that it aims to be 'revelation', not confusion! It makes use of Old Testament images and symbols from a type of writing known as 'apocalyptic'. This is rather like sci-fi which explores contemporary challenges by projecting them into a story set in the future.

Revelation starts with an amazing vision of Jesus in glory, the ascended Lord of all time, from beginning to end. This book seeks to encourage its readers by showing how in spite of appearances to the contrary, Jesus is Lord, both in the church and in the political world of the time.

Revelation looks at the horrors that are going on and reveals how God is at work to bring about the rule of Christ.

The opening vision of Jesus is followed by letters addressed to seven churches in Asia Minor which are listed in the order a traveller might come across them. Jesus shows his intimate knowledge of each church and its city and has a message to help each church to be faithful. That faithfulness takes different forms according to the situation (chapters 2–3).

Not only is Jesus Lord of the churches, but in heaven we see the reality of a universe where God's lordship is acknowledged in vast communal worship (chapters 4–7).The seeds of the next section are sown in these chapters. The Lamb (Jesus) alone can open the scrolls which permit the unfolding of history (all history is under the Lamb's control and he plays the pivotal role in it). The revealing of this history is a complex process involving the symbolic opening of seven seals; the final seal opens up into a series of seven new scenes, heralded by trumpets. The scene introduced by the seventh trumpet, in turn, seems to open up into yet another series of events recorded in chapters 12–18 and includes seven plagues. Rather than looking at a continuous time span, we are probably meant to envisage that we are looking through a series of lenses, each one providing more and more detail of the cosmic significance of history (seven is understood to be the number for totality). Terrible events are taking place on earth, but these are integrated with what is going on in the heavenly realm: the conflict between Satan and God.

John, the author of Revelation, is absolutely sure that the ultimate victory is with God (that is what crucifixion and resurrection prove), but he also wants the followers of Jesus to remain faithful during the violent tests of their faith on earth.

Fittingly, the book concludes with a vision of God's final triumph, the destruction of all evil and the creation of a new heaven and earth, at the heart of which is the reality of God.

Group discussion

In the light of Acts 2, divide the whole group into three sub-groups and ask one group to note what they discover about God the Father, another God the Son and the final one God the Holy Spirit. Each sub-group decides on five key points which are then shared with the whole group.

Bible encounter

Make two lists from the word cloud above (You have seen it already - see page 23)

1. those from the word cloud who appear in Hebrews 11
2. those in the word cloud but not in Hebrews 11.

Who would you like to add into Hebrews 11 as an example of living by faith – trusting the promises of God – from the characters mentioned in the word cloud?

Suggestions for reflection

Read Revelation 21. What excites you most about this description of God's new creation? What would you like to add to make your vision of the new creation even more complete?

Draw or paint (maybe in abstract or realist style) something which captures this vision of God's new creation. Alternatively, choose or even compose a piece of music which encapsulates this vision for you.

Key readings

Acts 2
Romans 5
Hebrews 11
1 Peter 1
Revelation 21

SESSION 5

THE DRAMA OF SCRIPTURE

By now you will have picked up something of the grand sweep of the Bible. It is a complex book or rather, as we have seen, a set of books; it spans not simply decades but millennia; it involves multiple genres, many authors and a myriad of voices. Yet, Christians believe that it has a profound unity which can deeply shape and enrich their lives. This is how they have experienced and benefited from engaging with the Bible respectfully, enquiringly and humbly. Above all it is a set of writings through which God chooses to reveal himself in a totally unique way. Christians also recognise that central to this sprawling collection of texts is the life, death, resurrection and impact of Jesus. To make the best sense of the Bible, we need to recognise the mission of Jesus as central. This enables us to read the Old Testament as moving towards Jesus and the life of the churches flowing from him. Take Jesus out of the equation and it no longer makes sense.

> The Word became a human being and, full of grace and truth, lived among us.
>
> John 1.14 (GNB)

It is fairly easy to make such an assertion, but much harder to establish it in detail and, most challengingly of all, answer the question of how individuals can express the message of Scripture helpfully and creatively for themselves and to whoever else they wish to commend the Bible. How could we approach this whole book – the Bible – in such a way that we can make good sense of it and live our lives in its light? Each generation has to discover its own answers to these vital questions. For many, perceiving the Bible in terms of a drama has proved very fruitful. This approach was first developed by Prof Tom Wright, former Bishop of Durham and a very effective communicator, apologist, and New Testament scholar. Since then many have followed him in exploring the 'drama' metaphor for the Bible. We will explain and apply it here. Thinking of this book as a drama might seem strange, but it proves to be a way to engage with the Bible in a richer way. We will also review what we discovered in the previous four chapters of this booklet.

Telling the story

Three common stories that shape most of us to some extent are:

- Human beings are essentially individuals, and we have the right to live our own lives (individualism).
- Making and spending money and getting things are the first priority for human wellbeing and give us our identity (consumerism).
- Violence is the only way to rescue nations and individuals from oppressors (the myth of redemptive violence).

Calling the Bible a drama is to apply a metaphor to the Bible. There are many metaphors that the Bible uses about itself, such as 'bread', 'light' and 'sword'. People have developed their own pictures for it too. Metaphors are important, because they engage our imaginations and emotions and enable us to live with complex truths in a positive and beneficial way. That is partly why the 'Drama of Scripture' is energising. Metaphors may be pictures, but they are also like lenses through which we can see further or see more detail.

An old hymn described the Bible as 'a book full of stories' ('God has given us a book full of stories' by Maria Penstone [1859-1910]). If we take 'stories' to mean fairy tales or trivial entertaining yarns, then such a picture can mislead us. If we understand this as a fairly random collection of exemplary literature from the past, it will also mislead. If, however, we define story as something full of character, interest and fascination, we are beginning to move towards the idea of drama. Drama builds on the understanding that the Bible is 'narratival', meaning that each of us and each of our communities tells a story to make sense of our lives, for instance when we explain why we did something or when introducing ourselves to someone. We share stories to reveal our identity and to build relationships. If we lose our memory, and thus our story, we feel very lost.

We all live by stories big and small that impact our lives.

We also encounter these through TV, advertisements, films and books.

Equally, when we engage with the big story of the Bible, it starts to influence our own personal life story. As we read a novel or see a film we enter into its 'narratival world' for a while and it shapes our feelings and attitudes. With the Bible we are invited to become part of its story, not for the time we are reading or watching and an hour or two after, but for a lifetime. Indeed the Bible offers a big story – the 'story of the world – from beginning to end. So it actually claims to be the true story of everyone and therefore to make proper sense of our individual stories as we find our place within it.

'Drama' is a dynamic way of telling a story through scenery, lighting, possibly music, and above all the actors' words, gestures and actions. Calling the Bible a drama helps us to recognise that we can look at it as a big story and that, like classical dramas, it can be divided into acts.

A five-act drama

There are five acts for the Bible:

1. Creation – sets the context for the whole drama: Genesis 1.1

2. The Fall – presents the disruptive element which the rest of the drama seeks to solve or unravel while introducing some of the main characters: Genesis 3–11

3. The Old Testament people of God: Israel – the outworking of the disruption and God's interventions to bring his salvation: Genesis 12 to Malachi

4. The Saviour – tension mounts as the one who will resolve the conflict is introduced: the Gospels

Classical Drama
In the second century BC, Roman dramatist Terence wrote plays in five acts and this form has dominated Western drama; it fits the unfolding of a long story well.

Act 1
Provides background information, introduces key characters and depicts the situation which is about to be destabilised.

Act 2
Introduces the conflict.

Act 3
The heart of the drama where the implications of the conflict and its intensification are depicted.

Act 4
Resolution of the conflict becomes inevtiable.

Act 5
The final act is the resolution and the re-establishment of order.

5. From the birth of the Church to the new creation – the re-establishment of order and the restoration of 'peace': Acts to Revelation.

There is more than one way of dividing the biblical drama into acts. Another book on the subject puts it like this:

1. God establishes his kingdom
2. Rebellion in the kingdom
3. The King chooses Israel: redemption initiated
4. The coming of the King: redemption accomplished
5. Spreading the news of the King: the mission of the church
6. The return of the King: redemption completed

(see C G Bartholomew and M W Goheen, *The Drama of Scripture – Finding our place in the biblical story*, SPCK 2004).

One benefit of seeing the Bible as a five (or six) act drama is that it provides a way of recognising that the whole library of biblical books makes up one coherent story. It also enables us to handle the deviations in the story line (these occur in any drama – perhaps a comic scene or maybe even some music, e. g. when the characters attend a concert). In the Bible there can be different types of material (the technical word is 'genre'), without them detracting from the story as a whole. Indeed they can add depth and variety to the big story. For example, the Psalms represent one such major detour; they immerse us in Israel's worship and often leave us with a song or two running round our heads that we re-use on other occasions. However, it is equally important that we don't forget the plot.

This perspective also helps us recognise that not everything said by every character represents the view of the author (whether the writer of the particular passage, or more significantly, God himself). There may be 'voices' within the drama which are diametrically opposite to the author's views and which serve to highlight them, and so it is with the Bible. Readers can learn to discern which is the true message. One way to do that is to wait to the end and see how the story unfolds.

There are two, final, really important points.

1. The principal actor

The first is that within the biblical drama the chief actor is God. Only to study the Bible for its grammar, history, ideology or to be fascinated only with secondary characters, even important ones like King David or Paul, is to misread it. The Bible is ultimately there to help people discover God, in the context of his interaction with and commitment to human beings and the life of the world. Once we get used to reading the Bible with the drama of Scripture in mind, we discern that it does not provide abstract theological principles but shows God interacting with us human beings.

2. The missing scene

The second point is that this drama has one scene missing! It is the penultimate scene in Act 5, which begins with the founding of the Church (see Acts of the Apostles); it goes on to give insights into the developing life of the Church (letters by Paul, Peter, James, John and others). It finishes with the end of this vast story. In Revelation and elsewhere, such as the Gospels and the letters, we are given hints and glimpses of the conclusion of the drama; through all that Christ has done God brings into existence a 'new heaven and a new earth' (Revaelation 21.1). Until then, from a Christian point of view, we are in the same 'time zone' as the early Church. We are part of the roll-out of the Gospel across the world following the death, resurrection and ascension of Christ and the giving of 'the promise from [his] Father' (Acts 1.4), the Holy Spirit.

As far as the Bible is concerned, the period in which we now live, and indeed the majority of the time since the end of the first century, is left blank. Like a group of Shakespearean actors who know something of the author and a lot about the drama we have to work out what could legitimately go on in the missing scene, taking into account the plot, the characters, the shape of the drama and above all its conclusion. In Tom Wright's words Christians are called to 'faithful improvisation' (NT wright, 2005, p93) living our lives within, and consistent with, the unfolding drama of the Bible. In other words, every person's story fits into the biblical story (no one can escape this!), and as Christians we seek intentionally to fit our lives into the story and contribute to it. Aided by the Holy Spirit, we work out how we should behave, live and believe, to help move the story towards its God-given ending.

> All the actors and all the travelling companies of which they are a part (i.e. different churches) are free to improvise their own fresh scenes. No actor, no company, is free to improvise scenes from another play or one with a different ending.
>
> (N T Wright, *Scripture and the Authority of God*, SPCK 2005, page 93)

This faithful improvisation (i.e. with innovation and consistency) of the penultimate scene in Act 5 enables us to respect the authority of God throughout Scripture, discern how we are to live in ever changing circumstances, understand why different Christians may come to different views about issues, and see our lives within the whole drama of Scripture that is the true story of the world. Living this way means to live biblically and Christianly in our own context, ensuring we allow God to direct us. Without this 'story' we will fall into living by one of the other contemporary stories (see text box, page 38)

We do not do this as isolated individuals; we need the other actors to help us. This is one reason why it is essential to belong to a community of Christians, people who are committed by and empowered to live within the Bible's drama. Thus, understanding the Bible as God's drama helps us make sense of the many parts of the Bible we noted in chapters 1–4. Knowing the whole story enables us to play our legitimate role in it.

Bible encounter

Look at this animated presentation of the five-act drama of the Bible:

http://pioneer.cms-uk.org/2011/07/01/the-story-of-everything/

Consider, on your own or in a group, what you like/dislike about the presentation.

1. What you would like to add to it from your engagement with this booklet?
2. Why not try this out with your home group, if you attend one, or even in a church service.

Suggestions for reflection

Think of an issue in your life you are wondering how to handle. This may be in the workplace, a family concern, a social topic, or a personal, moral dilemma. Then place yourself – with the concern – in the Drama of Scripture, Act 5, Scene 3. Of course use your mind, pray about the issue as you would with any other topic, seek for the insight of God's Spirit, search the Scriptures etc.; but also work out how to enact this situation with 'faithful improvisation'.

Group discussion

Share together from a book, film, TV soap, news bulletin or similar (at least one for each person) where the story has gripped your imagination and prompted you to feel, think and act differently. Try and help each other identify why it impacted you so much.

Identify key features of the biblical story which might reshape the way we live; consider where the biblical story runs counter to the stories of individualism, consumerism and redemptive violence (see text box page 38).

SESSION 6

THE 'XTRA' BOOKS

One of the strangest discoveries we can make about the Bible is that different Bibles have different numbers of books in them! Some have 66 (39 in the Old Testament and 27 in the New), others have up to 15 more.

Sometimes these extra books are all gathered together and appear between the Old and New Testaments and sometimes they are dispersed between the Old Testament ones. So, while the 'X' in 'Xtra' could stand for 'unknown at least to many' or 'additional', it is not for 'rejected' or 'wrong'!

These extra books are known as either the Apocrypha (which is the Protestant's preferred word) or the Deuterocanon (which is the Catholic preferred name for them). One of the main reasons as to why these books are included or not is whether the translation tradition is following the Hebrew Old Testament or the Greek one, known as the Septuagint (often indicated by LXX – this is the Roman numeral for 70 and there is an historic explanation of the translation into Greek which attributes it to 70 scholars).

People recognise that these additional books are of value in helping us understand how Jewish thinking was developing between the end of the Old Testament era and

The Deuterocanonical books
Tobit
Judith
Additions to Esther
Wisdom of Solomon
Ecclesiasticus (Wisdom of Ben Sirach)
Baruch
The Letter of Jeremiah
Additions to Daniel
1–2 Maccabees
1 Esdras
Prayer of Manasseh
3 Maccabees
4 Maccabees
Psalm 151

the beginning of the New. They also provide an account of the history of the period. Many Christians who know them recognise that they provide spiritual insights and perspectives that can enrich us but that these books are not primarily to be used for shaping our Christian thinking or doctrines. They use many genres and reflect an attempt to encourage Jews under persecution and pressure to resist both pagan idolatry and philosophy. They emphasise the sovereignty and provision of God, the superiority of his laws, but also often the compatibility with 'wisdom' which links them to some Greek philosophy. They also indicate how people in the last 300 years before Christ were engaging with their own older, Old Testament, traditions.

The history books: 1–4 Maccabees

As with both Old and New Testaments there are books which recount the history. These four books are rather different from each other and the common titling can be misleading.

The main ones for history are 1 and 2 Maccabees. They cover a very significant period in Jewish history, but in rather different ways. 1 Maccabees relates to 167–142 BC and describes how Jewish patriots gained liberation from pagan ruler, Antiochus IV, resisting his attempts to compromise their Jewish commitments. Judas initiated the revolt and his brother Simon combined the offices of Ruler and High Priest. 2 Maccabees, despite covering a similar historical period, has more theological interests and claims to summarize a larger work by Jason of Cyrene.

3 Maccabees is more like a historical novel and, confusingly, deals with the end of the 3rd century BC, telling how Egyptian Jews were delivered from Ptolemy IV. It is probably intended to encourage Alexandrian Jews to resist persecution through prayer and commitment to God's laws.

4 Maccabees is more philosophical. However, it uses 2 Maccabees 6–7 to help establish that wisdom is sovereign over emotions and based in the laws of God. From a Christian

Our answer to the word cloud
(see page 22)

Adam
Eve
Cain
Abel
Noah
Abraham
Lot
Isaac
Jacob
Joseph
Moses
Joshua
[Prophets]
Deborah
Ruth
Samuel
Saul
David
Solomon
Elijah
Elisha
Isaiah
Jeremiah
Ezra
Nehemiah
Esther
Ezekiel
Daniel
[Prophets]

perspective it is noteworthy that a martyr's suffering is presented as having power to atone for the sins of the whole people.

The wisdom books: Ecclesiasticus and Wisdom of Solomon

These are substantial writings. Originally written in Hebrew around 175 BC by Ben Sirach, Ecclesiasticus is a translation into Greek by the grandson of the author. Sometimes it is reminiscent of Proverbs, but it also provides a wonderful perspective as to how the Old Testament was viewed at this time. It eulogizes the famous ancestors, and emphasizes that true wisdom comes from God, not philosophy. The Wisdom of Solomon (probably written around 100 BC – AD 50) seeks to integrate Jewish wisdom with Greek thinking, in such a way as to show the superiority of Jewish wisdom. It is noteworthy for some important developments, including reflection on immortality for those who keep the Jewish faith (chapter 3) and a strong appeal to reject false, idolatrous religions (chapters 13–19). It also provides reflection on Israel's early history.

Other writings – Tobit, Judith and Baruch

Tobit is a fantastical tale of demons and angels, probably written around 180 BC. At its heart is encouragement to resist compromise with Greek culture and an emphasis on God's support for those who keep his laws.

Judith – the book – recounts how Judith, a devout widow, enables Jerusalem to escape from the siege of Nebuchadnezzar (wrongly thought to be Assyrian rather than Babylonian). She does this using her feminine ingenuity – perhaps showing the value of weakness rather than brute strength (compare 1 Corinthians 1.21–2.4). This story now forms the basis of the Jewish festival of Hanukkah.

Baruch seems to be a compilation including a long

confession of Israel's sin (1.16–3.8) and a poem rejoicing in God's wisdom (3.9–4. 4). It also includes a poem about God's restoration of Israel (4.5–5.9). Although set in the sixth century BC it is probably intended as encouragement to Jews in the diaspora (those who were living as permanent exiles around the Greco-Roman world).

Additions – the Letter of Jeremiah, Additions to Daniel and Esther, 1 Esdras, the Prayer of Manasseh, 2 Esdras, Psalm 151

The Letter of Jeremiah is a short piece based on Jeremiah 10.1–16. Often considered as chapter 6 of Baruch, it encourages resistance to the worship of idols.

Additions to Daniel and Esther: there are three additions in Daniel (The Prayer of Azariah, Susanna and Bel and the Dragon) and six in Esther (Mordeccai's dream, King Artaxerxes' letter, prayers by Mordecai and Esther, Esther's encounter with Artaxerexes, a letter from the king praising the Jews and the interpretation of Mordecai's dream). Together they might be an attempt to make the book of Esther more religious.

1 Esdras often offers an alternative to parts of Chronicles and Nehemiah, but 3.1–5.6 is unique. It recounts a debate between King Darius' bodyguards and leads to Zerubbabel (the Jewish bodyguard) receiving permission to rebuild the Temple in Jerusalem.

The Prayer of Manasseh is a reconstruction of the prayer he could have offered when he was exiled to Babylon (see 2 Chronicles 33.11–13).

Although 2 Esdras presents itself as referring to the destruction of the Jerusalem Temple in 587 BC, it is offering consolation for the destruction of the second temple in AD 70. It does this primarily through apocalyptic visions.

Psalm 151 is attributed to David and relates his selection by God to kill Goliath and become Israel's king.

Key readings

1 Maccabees 4

Ecclesiasticus (The Translator's Preface)

Ecclesiasticus 44

The Wisdom of Solomon 3

Tobit 6

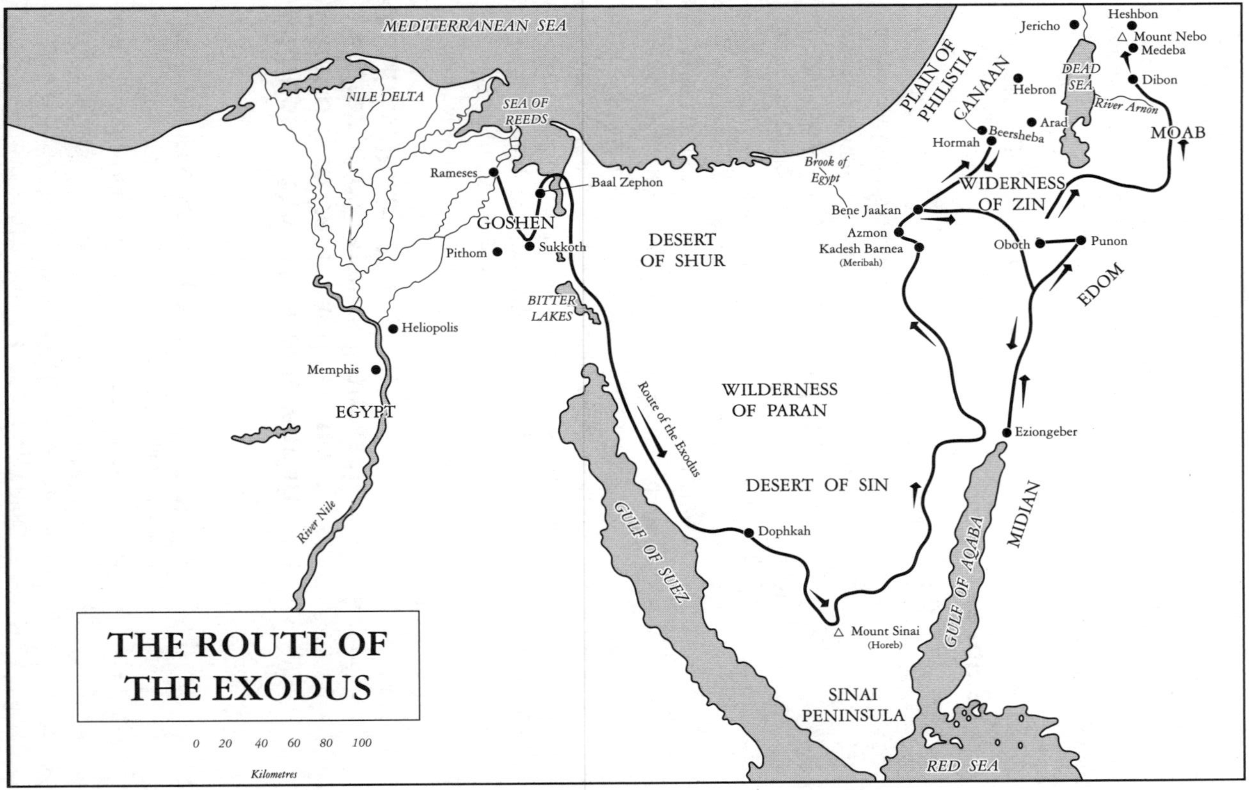
THE ROUTE OF
THE EXODUS
0 20 40 60 80 100
Kilometres
MEDITERRANEAN SEA
NILE DELTA
SEA OF REEDS
Rameses
Baal Zephon
GOSHEN
Pithom
Sukkoth
BITTER LAKES
Heliopolis
Memphis
EGYPT
River Nile
DESERT OF SHUR
WILDERNESS OF PARAN
Route of the Exodus
DESERT OF SIN
Dophkah
GULF OF SUEZ
Mount Sinai
(Horeb)
SINAI PENINSULA
GULF OF AQABA
RED SEA
MIDIAN
Eziongeber
Brook of Egypt
Bene Jaakan
Azmon
Kadesh Barnea
(Meribah)
PLAIN OF PHILISTIA
CANAAN
Hormah
Beersheba
Arad
Hebron
Jericho
DEAD SEA
River Arnon
Heshbon
Mount Nebo
Medeba
Dibon
MOAB
WIDERNESS OF ZIN
Oboth
Punon
EDOM